HUMAN

CONNECT THROUGH EMOTIONAL

INTELLIGENCE

To live in peace at work and home

NITIN DC

Ordering Information:

BookTrail Agency
8838 Sleepy Hollow Rd.
Kansas City, MO 64114

Printed in the United States of America

PREFACE

I am writing this book on my knowledge and experience gathered by following the principle of maintaining self-respect through honesty, sincerity, and goodwill for others.

I have been in various professions right from my graduation days, and I have seen success in my own way. The success that is revered through constant appreciation for the work I do, the respect I have consistently received from my managers, peers, subordinates, supporting staff, etc. Even in my personal life, I have been a person who has always tried to keep people together, help them, and support them despite the differences I have for them or they have for me.

I have played my role in the social cause by mobilizing people to do service for others and also making personal contributions in the best way I can to help and support people in need. In return, what I have received is a lot of adulation and support for what I do.

I have always believed that this is the wealth that I carry which is in a way my measure of success that I have gained in my life. I cannot call myself successful when it comes to my bank balance, although I have done considerably well, but what I enjoy wherever I go and whatever I do is tremendous amount of respect and goodwill from the people I work with.

I call it a failure in my life whenever I lose a friend or a well-wisher due to my negligence, arrogance, or for that matter, ignorance. So far I have not lost any of them due to my own doing. Yes, I don't stay in touch with all of them, but all of them know me as a person who is always giving and selfless which is itself is the biggest gain I have in my life.

So I decided to put it in the form of a book on everything I firmly believe and practice. I have a few idols for myself, and the most prominent amongst them is Gandhiji. I believe in service and sacrifice not to the extent that Gandhiji could do but to the extent that I can call myself a good human being.

I love people, and I yearn for people to love me. Just by having these attributes, I have reached a considerable level of success in my life and a lot of adulation, which I feel many others can also seek and get in their life.

I have never been depressed in my life since I have never considered my failures as a defeat. I have always seen it as an opportunity and worked my way through it. I only shed tears when I see or hear a sad story about others; when it comes to me and my life, I never cry. Instead, I start working through it.

My friends and my well-wishers regard me as a highly patient and passionate person; few of them also consider me smart, and also I have heard consistently from Indians and foreigners alike about my positive attitude towards life, the attitude and ability to appreciate others and see positive attributes in them while ignoring the negative aspects.

INTRODUCTION

This book is for any reader irrespective of the field of work or background they come from. It is a book written straight from the heart, relating to every bit of experience I could gather, in the course of my work and personal life.

The book has a simple tone to it, to understand and realize the concepts without any difficulty. It is all about bringing to attention those subtle aspects, which often may hit our blind spots, thereby creating awareness that can help our mind maintain peace.

Although I graduated in the field of Mechanical Engineering and worked as a Software Engineer post my certification from IBM in Advanced Software Engineering, my Post Graduation was in the field of Human Resources Management. After my Post Graduation, I have been working in the field of Human Resources for more than a decade, 14 years to be precise at Samsung Research. I found my niche as a coach, I now play the role of Master Coach for South West Asia region of Samsung and I am also a ICF certified Coach.

In my entire stint as a HR Professional, I have tried to master establishing Human connect, based on consistent success that I witnessed in building connections earlier in my role as Employee Relations specialist and now as a Master coach, I have done my bit in penning down the secret behind the success I had by the virtue of influencing through establishing Human connect.

Irrespective of my position in office whether I was a junior member or a senior. I have been able to influence leadership and employees in the organization building strong Rapport with 5 different Managing Directors and multiple CFOs, all of them were of Korean Origin and one of them being Indian both in India and Samsung Head Quarters in Korea. All this in a way represents my ability to bear influence through emotional connect by virtue of Emotional Intelligence using all approaches that are illustrated in the book.

Likewise in my brief stint as a self employed Business coach while I was living in New Zealand, I was able to register 15 clients in just 3 months, using the attributes of Human Connect through Emotional Intelligence.

DEFINITION

*I*n a very simple sense, emotional intelligence is to regulate one's own emotions and feelings to influence the other's emotional state.

Whenever we meet people, more often than not, we expect the other to be receptive to our emotional state. Since it is practically difficult to read the other's mind, we thereby rely on our own feelings about us and expect the other to know about it.

Well, that is the single most difficult task which today's scientist would want the most sophisticated and futuristic computer/robot to do. I don't think they have found a way yet.

Coming back to humans, as much as it is next to impossible for a machine to do, humans can still do it by putting a little effort.

So what does this effort involve?

1. Patience
2. Persistence
3. Ability to ask the right questions
4. Influence

Not the necessarily in that order.

(1) Patience

This is the first and foremost aspect of empowering yourself in the eyes of the other. As long as you are able to hear out the other person with immense patience, you have already gained the other person's respect towards you. It is very simple and basic.

There are many situations in your daily life where things do not go your way and you tend to lose your temper/mind and body control. Especially, when there is a very difficult situation, you might have heard of many techniques to deal with it. One such famous method is to count to ten when you get angry before you react or say anything. My way of doing it is by absorbing. Your strength lies in how much you can absorb. Many seem to have this misconception that when you are aggressive and attacking, you are tough; the truth is it makes you weak. Aggression makes you lose control over mind and body; however, there is a different from of aggression, which is patience through absorption. If you allow everything that happened to you sink in a relaxed manner, you automatically discover solutions to all your problems. Many say they do not have time; they can't sit and listen for hours together. Once again, this is just a misconception. One of my very intelligent friends used to tell me twenty-four hours is a lot of time, so don't count your days as day 1, day 2, etc. Count it as multiples of twenty-four hours, and in a year, you actually had $24 \times 365 = 8,760$ hours. This indeed is a lot of time. If your time is spent in thinking patiently, helping others by listening to them for hours, and keeping calm during difficult situations, your time is well spent. Many youngsters are taught that time is money and money is time. I have heard people talk about Bill Gates that if he actually bends down to pick up ten dollars, he has actually lost thousands of dollars, and that is the value of his time. Well, the fact of the matter is, Bill gates is actually spending a whole lot of his time going around talking to people who are in no way connected to his business but people who need his money without contributing anything back to his company's profit.

My point is that patience teaches you how to lead life in an effective manner by gaining people's respect rather than the superficial pride by being called as a man who is always busy.

However, it is not that easy; there could be several instances where the other person is suddenly not making sense and you are unable to connect with what the other person is saying. In such a situation, your patience may tend to wear out. The best thing to do at this stage is not to start talking, whereas ask the permission of the other person if you can interrupt. It may put off the other person if you start by saying, 'May I interrupt?' Although in many of the official meetings, this is an established protocol. However, it may not work very well when you are doing a personal interaction.

The better way to interrupt will be by actually apologizing for interrupting, saying that you are sorry to interrupt but then you have question to ask. Ask the question quickly to bring the context back into the conversation and allow the other person to continue.

(2) Persistence

It is very important that you persist with the mutual objective you have set out for when you begin with meeting the person. That objective has to be mutual in nature. For instance, when you start a conversation with a person, he has a particular objective in mind which he may not reveal unless he/she has established some level of trust in you, so you need to keep an open mind for the other person to build that trust in you. In one sense, you should not focus on your objective before you understand or get to know the objective of the other person. Once you are able to figure out what the other person is seeking in you, you should have an open mind to accept it without questioning it while you are already in your mind trying to map it or connect it with your objective.

Having accepted the objective of the other person, you have now gained his trust and attention towards you. You have to now move slowly towards expressing your objective while you have committed yourself in serving the other person's objective. It always works when you are instantaneous in accepting the other while you are more subtle in expressing your own objective; this way, you will be able to establish a deep-rooted connection by not allowing your objective to override the other.

Once you have successfully established the connection, you need to work hard towards not only getting your objective achieved but also ensuring the other person has his/her stake in it. If you back off or you do not want to put the effort in following up with the other person in the quest of achieving the objective set by each one of you or you drain out, it may lead to a situation where you have to go through the entire process of establishing the connection all over again. So before you start, you tend to drain out.

(3) Ability to Ask the Right Question

One of the most important attributes to have while establishing a connection with people is the ability to ask the right question. Usually in the course of a conversation, it is very natural for the conversation to drift. In some cases, some people have the social compulsive disorder of going on and on where there is no stopping. In either situation, it is important to bring the context back into the conversation, else the conversation will become an utter waste of time. The interaction I am talking about can apply to any situation. Be it an interview, casual talk in the airport or an airplane, an official discussion, etc. In order to bring the conversation back into context, it is very important to ask the right question. Asking a question may sometimes be a bit tricky since the other person may take it offensively if the right question is not asked although it was not intentional. Here are some tips about how to ask the right question.

1) Even though what the other person is saying is not making sense to you, don't say that. I mean, you should not say, 'You are not making sense to me', although it is the right thing to say.

2) Instead, you can use a more productive approach of asking questions which connects to the story that the other person is telling. In a sense, ask a question which makes the other person trust that you are listening to him/her.

3) For example, when the conversation started to discuss about two politicians and you want to make your point on who is better and in the course of it the other person drifts into talking about caste religion and which is the better religion, the question you can ask could be 'Wait a minute, are we talking about the religion of these politicians?' The other person will suddenly remember the context and in reciprocation will respond by saying, 'No, I was talking about the kind of people who vote for these politicians', so your next question could be 'Do you mean that these politicians try to influence a particular religion?' Now you can see what is happening; you are slowly bringing back the other person to talk about the two politicians instead of two religions.

Likewise there could be several instances where you can interrupt a conversation by asking the right questions to bring the conversation into context. This is no rocket science, but the difficult part is to handle your emotions in the course of doing this. Since often such conversations involve a lot of faith, belief, and thereby emotions induced in it. So if the question is not asked in the right spirit or if the question is asked to somehow make the other person feel that he/she is not making great sense and thereby you want to end the conversation, it may actually start causing a drift in the relationship rather than just a conversation. Often in the West, people are more direct; they don't want to beat around the bush, so they rather say a very simple and straightforward statement which is 'It just does not make any sense.' Now this causes an immediate drift in a person's feelings about the other, and as this intensifies, they stop talking to each other and over a period of time even stop meeting each other.

So in the West, it is highly impractical for two people to stay together when they are just not making sense to each other, whereas in most of the Asian countries especially in India, relationships are highly emotional in nature. Even if the other person is not making any sense, we tend to stick along with the conversation either by being patient, not showing any frustration and handling it subtly, or by asking the right questions in such a way that the other person does not feel hurt by it.

Let us take another example where we can take two such scenarios with people deeply engrossed in a conversation. We shall create an intrusion in both these scenarios: one of the intrusions would end up in drifting the conversation apart, thereby causing a friction between the two people, and the other, where one person is saying something that is not acceptable, yet their conversation does not break and it ends up in a positive conclusion to the conversation.

Scenario 1 Conversation that Causes Conflict

Two people, Alex and Rakshit, are trying to decide a location for a trip with their common friends. Both are very good friends and are always well known to lead the troupe whenever and wherever they plan for a trip. So both are friendly rivals trying to maintain an edge over the other. So Alex starts by saying, 'I think we have done enough of beach side trips, this time let us try hill station.' So he starts with his monologue on what they all could do there. He is doing this before he finds out what is there in Rakshit's mind. Now Rakshit is a bit weary, and he is not paying attention. Suddenly while Alex is asking a question related to whatever he started with, Rakshit starts mumbling, saying that he is not sure. Alex quickly realizes that Rakshit is not paying attention. Now he starts a new argument, stating that 'You think you know a better place.' Rakshit responds by saying, 'How about going to some place very cool, where we don't burn in the hot sun?' This is the beginning of the drift. Instead of just stating his desire while he was given a chance, out of sheer frustration Rakshit happens to involuntarily taunt Alex's idea. Now Alex, instead of trying to pick what exactly Rakshit's idea is, he picks on the taunt which Rakshit made by telling him, 'What do you mean burn in the hot sun? I am talking about having fun at the beach, and everyone wants a tan at the end of the day.' So the argument would go on with Rakshit responding to Alex's argument telling him that it is only his assumption that people want a tan.

Scenario 2 Conversation that Converges and Results in an Amicable Solution

Two people, Alex and Rakshit, get together to decide on a trip. Alex starts by telling Rakshit that lie has a good place in his mind; however, lie also tells Rakshit to start first. Rakshit, eager to let Alex know what lie has in his mind and also glad that Alex told him to speak first, begins by saying that lie knows a place which is a hill station that has rivers, streams, and lot of trekking where they could also camp and have a campfire in the night. Suddenly, Alex kind of begins to like the idea, hearing all that Rakshit has to say about the place and the campfire—who would not like a campfire? Despite this, lie still wants to put across what lie has in his mind and look for Rakshit's reaction, so lie starts by saying, 'How about going to the beach that is not too far away from the place you suggested? There is a cruise in the night, and in the cruise, there is a night party with song and dance, and eventually the cruise will take us to a nearby island where we could camp, and during the day, we can go trekking up the river, have some fun boating, and return back for a campfire.' Now, Rakshit is way too excited, but lie has a question. He asks him whether it is true that they are going to camp in the island. So Alex says that it is not part of the trip, but it is actually possible to do that since the cruise will return the next day which is not a holiday, and they will have a chance to go back in the cruise as there will be no rush. He says this came into his mind only after hearing about what Rakshit had in his mind. Well then, Rakshit is absolutely excited, and he says it works perfect for him. This way they could play in the beach, camp in the night, and also enjoy the trekking. Eventually, it all works fine, and it ends into a perfect conversation which has an objective and converges into a decision which is consensual.

Lessons

1) It always works well if you are a good listener; it helps in effective communication.

2) Try to give an opportunity for the other person to speak; whenever you have your own idea to express, you may actually improvise your idea based on the other person's opinion.

3) It is always important to keep an objective in mind rather than an opinion since opinions can differ; as long as the objective is

the same, which is having fun in the above example, two opinions can converge to meet the objective.

4) By giving importance to the other's opinion, you make your own opinion stronger.

Bottom Line

Communication is an art, not a science; as long as you are able to measure up yourself in the eyes of others, you become an effective communicator.

In simple words, 'Learn to listen before you speak'.

It is easier said than done; it requires a lot of effort, but as long as you practice, it will become a habit.

(4) Influence

Building Rapport through Good Relationship

There are many elements that can nurture influence since influence is the most powerful quality that one can have that will transform him/her into a great leader rather than a blind follower. It is also something that can empower people bereft of position and fiscal status.

I have mentioned below several aspects that help in mastering the art of influence.

Now we have learnt a bit about how to have an effective conversation, let us talk about how to bear influence over others, which many great leaders have achieved and many good leaders aspire for to become a great leader.

I would like to talk about influence by taking examples of some of the great leaders of the yestergeneration. The best and the easiest example is Mahatma Gandhi. Mohandas Karamchand Gandhi, who is popularly known as Mahatma Gandhi, was a highly influential leader. His leadership did not involve any power or authority. He was neither a politician nor a dictator, yet he bore influence over millions of Indians who followed him and his principles. They loved him and affectionately called him bapu.

What was the secret of the unique Influence this man had over people? Well, the answer is very easy and simple. It was his simplicity. His actions spoke louder than words; however, his words had a strong influence over people since he practiced what he preached. To bear influence over others, the most important aspect is to practice what you preach; eventually what you gain by this is trust. People trusted Mahatma Gandhi more than their own kith and kin. Even to this day, people all over the world follow his principles of non-violence to make this world a better place to live. He actually told people that by resorting to non-violence, you can defeat the wickedest enemy since the enemy is seen as a friend and eventually the enmity turns into friendship.

So the key to bear influence over people is to win their trust, and let me tell you, it is very difficult to earn trust since earning trust may take ages while losing it takes just a moment. So in the quest of earning trust, we have to make sure that we do not lose it in one moment while it was built over the years. Usually in a husband and wife relationship, why do couples resort to divorce after spending many years living together? The simple answer is, while they have spent years together trying to earn the trust from each other, one argument based on a series of unrelated events can result in making this harsh decision which has a bad influence not only on them but on the other people who depend on them. However, sometimes it could also be for the better. It can only work out to be better when there is an attempt to keep a relationship which is not based on trust. To avoid keeping up with a relationship that is bequeathed of trust, the best thing is to declare that there is no trust and go for a mutual divorce. But more often than not, this isn't the case.

How do we earn trust, and how do we avoid breaking it?

Once again there is a very simple approach towards it—just do the right thing. Although it sounds that simple, many people falter since they try to be judgemental about what is right. This happens depending on the relationship each one of us maintains with the other. If the relationship is deep like a blood relation, we tend to forgive each other even if we don't do the right thing and end up in knots which invariably becomes difficult to get out of So the drift in relationship happens while we try to stand by each other based on false relationship rather than trust. Irrespective of the relationship that you maintain, if you give due regard to what is right, you will be able to judge a person better and invariably bear a strong influence on others. As long as one is able to insulate from relationship and build it on the basis of trust earned by clearly differentiating right from wrong, that relationship will last forever.

It is very important to keep one's moral ground high to earn trust of others and eventually bear influence on others.

Chapter II

VIRTUE OF BEING RIGHT

The guidance to good life is to follow the path of righteousness. We often see it in movies, read it in history books, fiction, etc. that there is this person who always does the right thing and he fights against the evil who follows the wrong path.

Why would people follow the wrong path? Is it consciously done, or is it unconscious or unintended? Many times human beings are victims of circumstances. If you put a person in an extreme situation where the choice is limited, he/she tends to break down and eventually ends up doing wrong. Now, is it possible to be right all the time? It is a very difficult proposition. Nobody can be 100 percent right; however, they can always intend to be right. The best way to handle situations so that the situations do not overpower you is by following the right path. By doing this, you will be able to lead things in such a way that even when you encounter a desperate situation, you will be able to control it and handle it to an extent that it does not take over you. For example, financial crisis—who does not have financial crisis? Each one of us goes through it at some stage of our lives, maybe not all. Whenever we are in a situation like this, more often people may resort to begging, borrowing, or stealing. When begging and borrowing is not working, the only other way is to steal. However, there is one other way which people don't try to explore during extreme situations—this is planning. When things are in bad shape, you should start planning, save every penny you earn, do compromises with your life and lifestyle, and give it some time until you completely recover.

Likewise, people may also encounter extreme situations in relationships, whether it is between husband and wife, siblings, parents, friends, etc. Quite often, people resort to abusing each other, not talking to each other, hurting each other. Often people resort to such behaviours to prove their righteousness. Well, the simple fact is that if you are right, you do not have to prove it to others; just do the right thing and be convinced. You do not have to go one step ahead to prove it to others. Often misunderstandings happen due to change in behaviours. When a person is used to another person behaving in a particular manner and suddenly that behaviour changes, there arises suspicion and the immediate reaction is changing behaviours against each other. To ensure that it does not lead into extreme situation, the best way to handle it is by maintaining your true self despite changes in behaviour by the other person. Whether the other person likes it or not, one need not change his/her behaviours due to the negative vibes or change in attitude of the other person due to some unforeseen reason. When you maintain to be right while the other is doing all kinds of mistakes in proving he/she is right, the other person ends up in knots and gets worried that he/she is losing a true friend since they realize that the changes are happening only within him/her while the other person is just the same.

Everyone appreciates being right, so why be wrong? We should not submit to situations and make ourselves unbecoming. We have to maintain our true nature despite various situations and circumstances that we encounter in life. That is when people will start believing in you and trust you come what may. Doing the right thing will also induce fearlessness; you do not have to fear anyone for doing something that is right and just.

There could be situations that you may encounter where you have to do something that your superior or your elder does not like. Many times people get into a dilemma whether to do the right thing or do what the boss/superior/elder says. If you fearlessly do the right things, your boss/superior/elder may not like it initially, but when you are able to maintain it, they will fail to overpower your guile and perseverance and will come under tremendous pressure to support and appreciate you since, as long as you are in the right path, others are able to see it and you will be able to gain over the other person irrespective of who the other person is in terms of seniority or position.

Chapter III

HUMAN VALUES: LEARN TO APPRECIATE AND HAVE A SENSE OF ACHIEVEMENT

The more you tell about it, the less it seems. Since humans are social beings. We live in a society where there is so much of diversity in the way we live, the language we speak, the customs we follow. More often than not, the custom, language, religion, etc. seem to be defining the characteristic of a particular human being in terms of their behaviours. Well, the way to look at it is not to be too self-righteous, saying that you cannot be influenced by any of these factors. In ancient times when human beings lived in the forests, they formed tribes, and each tribe was different from the other based on the way they look, way they interact, and their rituals. Often they used to fight wars against each other since it was survival. They always felt threatened by the other tribe in terms of sharing resources and following custom and tradition. The only way they could settle it since they could not understand each other's language and hence could not communicate was by killing each other.

In the recent history, we all know about the two world wars that were fought. Although it seemed slightly complicated as far as the reason for these wars to have been fought, the main factor still is each country and its leaders preached self-righteousness, claiming that they are right and the others are wrong. Probably the reason for this, unlike the ancient tribes where they could not fully understand each other's culture and tradition, is that the human race had become more intelligent and was able to communicate better with each other. However, people got into fanaticism, preaching that they were more superior to others although they really had not made a conscious attempt to find out about the others whom they felt they are more superior to.

Today, the world is maturing, although not completely. People are realizing that fighting or killing each other results in unnecessary destruction, so why not live together by sharing the better of each other? This led into a civilized society where education took precedence over mastery. It has given way to a more orderly way of living where everyone is trying to learn from each other and live a better life rather than die a hero for a few people. Yet we are not completely absolved of hating each other or committing crimes. The reason for this is also very simple. It is the lack of ability to appreciate someone who can be better than you and also maintain humility when you are better than others. We talk about healthy competition, but we are not able to practice it in its true spirit all the time. Yes, indeed it is easier said than done. It is not easy to appreciate others when you are in distress.

The best way to do it is try to work out what is good for you and not compare your achievements with others. One should consider it his/her achievement when one is able to rise up in his own eyes rather than for others. For example, if you have a friend or a neighbour who has a better living than you could ever have since he/she was fortunate to get a better education, support, etc., rather than feeling distressed that you were not fortunate enough to get that, it will be easier for you to look within yourself and figure out what is best for you, what is it that makes you happy, rather than thinking how the other person you admire would want to see you. When you try answering all those questions, wherein you probably might say now that you don't have a great education, do not try doing what the other person you admire can do best. Instead, explore something that you are good at and try to specialize in that and achieve a level of expertise that makes you feel confident that you have learnt enough to tell the world what you can do best. This requires years of effort, patience, and perseverance. In the course of your learning and development, you cannot still avoid coming across others who could be doing better than you. What is more important for you during this stage is to be patient and wait for your time.

When it is time for you, it may not be time for others like you. They will also feel the same way that you felt while you were in the course of achieving something. You should always remember that there cannot always be a gold medal, a trophy, or an article about you in the newspaper which spells your success. If you consider even a small word of praise from your friend, neighbour, well-wisher, and your own family as an achievement, then your life is much better lived. Since each one of us cannot be a hero, we need competition in life, and if the competition is healthy, the winner and the loser do not really matter. A person who loses a contest and feels that he gave more than 100 percent but at the end of the day lost against a better opponent is more at peace than a sore loser who felt the other did not really deserve to win.

What do you call such a thing? It is called sense of achievement. Like they say, it is good to have a sense of humour. Having a sense of achievement is even more important. Whoever has this never fails in what he/she is striving to do since he/she always pursues things with a goal in mind, and whoever has a goal will also have a sense of achievement. You can always rewrite your goals based on situations and circumstances, but do not do it for the fear of not achieving your goal. Even if you fail in achieving your goal, the process you followed in working towards it is by itself an achievement. This way you can extend your goal and still achieve it.

Chapter IV

PATH TO SUCCESS: HONESTY, SINCERITY, AND SELF-CONFIDENCE

Honesty

In today's world, the most necessary evil is to lie. Some people lie since they want to get the better of others, some do it since they want to save themselves from embarrassment, some people lie to escape from the crime they committed, and some people actually lie to save the other person they like. Does that mean that lies have become an integral part of our lives, something like a necessary evil where we cannot live without it? Having said that, the fact of the matter is most people lie for the fear of telling the truth. So can a calculated lie replace the truth? We have heard from the ancient epic Mahabharata where Lord Krishna, an embodiment of truth, had to lie on several occasions to correct the situation and make the good win over the evil. Well, it is an epic written illustrating something that may have happened thousands and millions of years ago. It is about faith and belief. Yet in India many of us have read it and also believe it happened.

There is nothing wrong in belief, but everything goes wrong when people start perceiving that it is OK to lie, since God himself lied, instead of introspecting what the author was trying to tell—Krishna had a role of saving the world, and he was the almighty who has to lead the world into the right end. Now coming to the point, can a lie replace the truth since it is told in the course of achieving something good? Maybe yes, maybe no. The simple aspect that we need to remember is how can we train ourselves? We have to tune ourselves in telling the truth all the time and lie sometimes when it comes to life and death and that a good lie has to be told only when it is needed to make things better or save a life. Despite doing it, it should be obvious to everyone that a lie has been told to save a life or make life better. This is the only time when a lie gets the better of truth. But the path that everyone has to follow is the path of truth; this way neither you will be in self-doubt nor will you mislead others. On the contrary, truth becomes an embodiment in you, and it will become very easy to earn the trust of people—too easy and too fast since you are an honest person.

Chapter V

MAINTAIN HUMILITY, BE HUMAN, DO NOT BECOME THE POSITION THAT YOU HAVE

Right from the day we are born, we are consistently and continuously influenced by various members around us in the society. Each one bears a different influence on us. For example, while we are kids, we seek for love and forgiveness from our parents and support from our siblings. As we grow up, we seek friendship from our parents and siblings, and once we have children, we start giving what we used to seek. In the process, we are in the cycle of relationship. In the whole process, we do not cease to be what we are—that is being human.

However, in this process, we tend to get influenced by situations in life and react to it adversely and sometimes forget our real self. This usually happens in the school life, college life, and eventually work life. After being taught all the good things by our parents and teachers, we come across a host of other people who are bred from a different environment, and in the course of interacting with them and handling situations, we tend to forget certain moral values that we have to maintain as a human being. We are immersed in the valley of desire, and we struggle to come out of it. In the course of achieving success, many of us try to find the easy way out and meet obstacles which we cannot handle.

How do we handle situations and achieve success by keeping our morality high?

It is again very simple but needs a lot of effort and willpower. The simple rule is to remember Maslow's hierarchy. As Maslow clearly defined in his studies, it will take a while for us to cross different stages of our life starting from physiological needs to safety, love/belonging, self-esteem needs, eventually reaching self-actualization. If we get stuck in any one of the initial stages, that is exactly when we cease to maintain human values. We fail to achieve the success or goal we desire. For example, someone who believes only by making money he/she can gain the respect of others is stuck in the stage of need for self-esteem in Maslow's hierarchy. At the same time, someone who is looking for a companion and does not have one or lost one will get stuck in the stage of love and belongingness. When they are stuck in any one of these stages in Maslow's hierarchy of needs, human beings fail to reach the moral high ground. They struggle through it and try to find their way out by adopting unacceptable means and end up destroying themselves by getting isolated.

It is necessary to reach the stage of self-actualization for achieving success by keeping high moral grounds. When a human being is able to handle physiological, safety, love/belongingness, self-esteem needs, he/she is able to attain the level of self-actualization that he desires. He/she will have the capability of seeing within than seeking others help in telling them who they are and what they are. Discover your own self and understanding yourself better than any others is basically self-actualization. However, it is easier said than done. Situations and circumstances can go against us. Despite this, if a person is able to give it some time and regain his composure to continue living the life of purity, honesty, and sincerity, it is possible to realize self-actualization. Self-actualization also means you have a sense of purpose for your living. You know what you represent and you are confident of achieving what you seek for since you have chosen the right means and you are along the right path to achieve it. When a person knows where he is going despite the uncertainties of tomorrow, then he/she has reached self-actualization. For such a person, life is not a puzzle; it is just a sequence of events. He/she will handle each of these events to its merits and will never get bogged down by it.

However, this needs a lot of patience and willpower. None of the needs has to trouble you to an extent that you are thinking hard about it and worried about how to satisfy that need. As much as it is a struggle and not easy to maintain high levels of morality, one should not compromise on it on the word go. It is OK if it takes time, but never use shortcuts to achieve it, and this will be the secret of your success.

Also in the course of achieving success, people attain different positions in life where a lot of responsibility and authority is vested on them. Now this position attained should not be the representation of the person; the person should remain the same as what he/she used to be as an innocent child who could never be influenced since as a child, everyone was innocent, pure, and honest. The moral values learnt should be the same at every stage. The person irrespective of the position should love others and be loved and respected by others. This particular aspect will help in continuing to remain successful and achieve great things in life.

Chapter VI

SIMPLICITY AND HUMILITY

The best example of a great leader who was simplicity and humility personified is once again Mahatma Gandhiji. He was one great man who led the nation just by the virtue of simplicity and humility. Well, not all of us can emulate this great man, but we can always adopt some of his principles which can help earn a lot of success and also provide personal satisfaction of loving people and being loved by them.

To be simple is not to shred the luxuries and the lifestyle. Being simple means to be simple in thoughts and actions. Often we encounter situations which get complicated due to the complex nature of the people around you. If you are successful, you definitely have competitors who are also trying to be successful and get the better of you. Not all of them may have a healthy way of doing it. Some of them may develop an inferiority complex and thereby attack you at every possible opportunity. The best way to counter it is to make the other person realize how his/her actions are not affecting you and make it evident that it is causing their own self-destruction when it comes to upholding moral value. You could achieve this is by being simple and not be too calculative.

If you start getting calculative about people, thinking about them all the time and countering every move, you will lose focus. This will lead you to a situation where your life is dependent on the other person who is bothering you. Despite facing the attacks by the other person, the best way to defend is by making the other person know that his actions do not worry you or bother you, rather it only makes you wonder what the other person is trying to achieve by it since you do not want to compete the other person with regard to each other's personality and character. Everyone is bound to have their own character. However, if something is not right about it and is affecting you, the best way to counter it is by letting the other person know about it and realize it. Like they say, 'Defence is the best form of attack'.

Humility

When it comes to humility, it is again easier said than done. Human beings are victims of desire, and as we all know, 'Desire is the cause for destruction'. As we grow in our lives, we tend to amass wealth and in the process become very important in the eyes of others. The materialistic wealth that attracts us will sometimes drift us from reality. While we interact with our counterparts, friends, and relatives, somewhere at the corner of the mind, the wealth, fame, and other aspects start ruling over your conscience, and you may tend to behave in a manner that is not the real you. You may have observed many people at high positions not meeting eye-to-eye with people, not smiling, just walking away if they are not too interested in the conversation, not mixing with staff who are lower in rank, etc. Although this seems to be a common behaviour, it may not be the right behaviour.

So how to maintain humility despite achieving high ranks in office. The best way to do it is by seeking love rather than respect. When you seek love of people, it does not matter who they are and what their rank is. One important aspect here is the more people love you, the more they respect you, and they also realize that the relationship they have with you is of love and nothing else. This way you will learn to command respect rather than demand it. This concept applies to your household as well. If you want your spouse/children to respect you when you cannot give them enough love, then you are demanding it from them, and what you get is hollow respect where there is no essence of love in it. This kind of relationship will turn out to be very fragile and break any time.

So the secret of maintaining humility with people is to love them and not just seek respect from them. Of course some people may not deserve it when they try to harm you or hurt you for vested interests. In such a situation, the best way to handle such people is not by isolating them but by keeping them close to you and making them realize that it does not affect you much what they think about you. You will not be repulsive or react to them for every instance they attack you, rather you will try to let it go past you, making it ineffective.

Also, we are a nation where people of the stature of Mahatma Gandhi ruled our hearts and minds and that of millions around the world. He was person who was humility personified; lie can be taken as an example where stature does not mean arrogance. You can be humble and have millions and billions following you. Of course in your day-to-day life, it will not be about people following you; it will be more to do with people liking you and willing to associate with you.

When you are facing challenges where you feel that you are a victim of political or selfish motives, the best way to counter it is by being bold and humble, so humility does not mean taking it all and not fighting against bad things. It actually means since you are trying to follow the right path, be bold yet don't lose humility and show arrogance; even a victim who plays arrogant can actually hurt someone.

Chapter VII

BE HONEST
TO YOURSELF
BEFORE YOU SEEK
FROM OTHERS

On many occasions since we are emotional beings who can express emotions loud and clear, we tend to seek justification for anything that goes against us. Having said that, let me also say that it is quite natural to be that way. It is not a crime, and it does not make anyone look greedy or selfish to seek justice. At the same time, it is very important to look within; it only requires a slight pause and do a little bit of soul-searching to figure out if what we are seeking is in conjunction with what is right to seek. Sometimes, the convenience factor always creeps in where you want the justice your way. It could be due to the fact that you are pressurized due to some of your own personal situations which are forcing you to seek justice to handle that situation. Well, it may happen sometimes that it could solve your personal situation eventually; however, if you do not see it in the broader frame of mind, it will definitely hit you back since fingers will be pointed and questions will be asked when a similar situation transpires with someone else and that person is seeking justice for which you do not agree since he/she is trying to handle his/her own personal situation.

The most simple and best way to handle this is by questioning yourself before questioning others, seeking answers within w.r.t. how to handle your personal situation. While you put an effort towards that and eventually be able to handle and sort your personal situation, you can then look outside with clear glasses rather than coloured glasses.

This way, you will never be caught with your foot in the mouth as the expression goes or become the accused in the course of accusing something that is not right. Like the saying goes, 'Don't throw stones at others while you live in a glass house'.

Chapter VIII

LIVE YOUR DREAMS

Who does not have dreams? Not the dreams that you get naturally while you sleep, the dreams we set for ourselves. The dreams that give momentum to our lives. A dream is one such aspect that does not choose who can have it. Every single human being—be it a child, teenager, young, and old—can have their own dreams. Rich and poor don't matter; dreams can take a coveted place in everyone's life.

So do dreams have to be realistic, achievable, and calculated? Not really, dreams can be wild, vivid, and out of this world. The more outreaching they are, the better it is since if you dream small, you will end up doing less, thinking less about yourself, and eventually underachieving.

There are many instances in the history of mankind where a person who hardly had any means to do what he wanted to do dreamt about it and eventually achieved it. When you keep your dreams larger than life, you will tend to push hard beyond your inherent capabilities and try to achieve more than what you think you are capable of You keep challenging yourself and increasing your bar and thereby realizing your true potential. Sometimes for some people, there is just no barrier; they keep pushing their bar so high that they end up achieving the unachievable. However, there are very few who are like this. But there can be many who dream and push their bar high and achieve what they wanted to and show it to the world how they could do it.

One important aspect about dreams is, all dreams need not end up in becoming wealthy, having riches, enjoying name, fame, etc.; the most successful dreams are the ones that have a sense of purpose. As long as there is a purpose to your dreams, you will rejoice when you fulfil your dreams even though it does not bring wealth, name, or fame. When it comes to name and fame, they are only incentives that you get alongside the actual earning of sense of pride and achievement. As far as wealth is concerned, there is no end to it; the more you have, the more you want. So it can never give you fulfillment or satisfaction.

Dream of what you want to be rather than what somebody else is. Rediscover yourself at every stage of working towards realizing your dreams. It will, on the whole, make you a better person. You will begin to trust yourself more than anybody else, which will earn you self-confidence. When the chips are down, the best way you can stand tall is by trusting your own instincts. In the course of achieving your dreams, if you do everything right in trusting your own instincts and goodwill and not follow ill advice of others, you will one day achieve your dreams.

Pursuit of dreams is the key to achievement of success; do not set a time limit for achieving it. There could be obstacles, which may deviate you from working towards it, so you cannot put a time frame for achieving your dreams. However, you will still achieve your dreams if you overcome the obstacles. Give it the time it takes and keep on with your pursuit.

At the end of the day, what matters is the course you take to achieve your dreams. When you have done all the right things in pursuit of your dreams, that itself is part of your achievement and fulfilling your dream is just a certificate of all your achievements.

Ultimately the most important key to success is living your dreams.

Chapter IX

EMPATHY

Although the word is simple and contains just seven letters in it, it is one of the strongest attributes that one can have to bear an influence over others, and the more genuine it is, the more fruits it bears. The word empathy basically means to think from the other's point of view/to put yourself in the other person's shoes and realize what is going on in the other person's mind. However, to empathize is not to show sympathy, they are actually two different sides of the same coin. When you show sympathy, you are feeling sorry for the other person. However, when you show empathy, you are actually putting your mind deep into the other's mind, trying to feel what the other person is feeling. What this does to the other person is quite phenomenal. Since you are able to feel what he/she feels, the other person will start believing in you; there is a sense of trust that is established. It transforms itself into a strong bond of faith and reassurance; it brings a sense of understanding between the two people which remains unbroken. The wavelength of thought is so well balanced that two people start feeling secured in the company of each other.

So it is important to have a sense of empathy when you want to help others/solve their problems.

Now the question arises, how do you do that? The basic rule is never feel sorry for the other person to the extent that you feel helpless; you should look deep and find out why the person has problems rather than just knowing what it is and feeling sorry for it. When bad things happen to people, we all sympathize and wish them well; however, we also feel helpless that we cannot do anything to help them. However, when you show empathy, there is a strong desire within you to solve the issue or problem the other person is facing by not just feeling sorry for it. You are looking for action rather than plain words that soothe the person. In the process, what happens is that the other person will also feel that his problem is solvable and gains self-confidence since other people are able to relate to it and can see that it can be solved.

Let us take an example. I think almost all of us at various levels face some sort of financial crisis. We are all bound by desire, a desire which overrides caution and in the process ends up intertwined and we fall into the debt trap. This leads into emotional crisis, which is sometimes unbearable since it has various legal consequences. You may have heard many stories of different types where people are going through a very bad phase in their life. When we choose not to help, the best we could do is to sympathize with the situation. However, if you show empathy, then you can actually reason out the cause for the crisis and advise a suitable solution. Let us say someone comes to you and tells you that he/she is in a debt trap and is about to face legal consequences. This will destroy the family as his/her child will be out of school and his/her partner in the house is not well and therefore cannot work to make ends meet. The worst is that he/she will have to face legal consequences, and the only way to avoid it is by selling everything he/she has. Despite that, he/she may not actually get out of the debt trap. Now when you are faced with such a situation, the best many could do with that person is show sympathy since it is too deep a crisis. However, if that person is a friend/well-wisher/close relative, you may not choose to wish away yourself from the crisis that the other person is facing. The best way to deal with it is to show empathy and talk to the person to understand the cause and effects of the crisis. The questions you may choose to ask would be how did it happen, what is the extent of the person's damage, and could the person provide all the details of the financial status. When you ask such questions, the other person will at least feel relieved that someone is able to look beyond the crisis and asking for more information. Once you have the information in hand, you have to probe more in terms of the means in which the person can repay and the time frame it needs. What is happening here is you have given a channel for the person to think and plan and then you have to provide encouragement by quoting instances of other people who were into such crisis and how they were able to get out of it. The best way to come out of a crisis is to think through it and plan, which the person who is in crisis would never do naturally. When he/she is forced to do it, then they will start thinking beyond the crisis and stop sulking over the crisis and start doing something in action.

Chapter X

HAVING A POSITIVE ATTITUDE

Positive attitude goes a long way in keeping control of your emotions. When you have a positive attitude towards life, life becomes more and more simple to deal with. Most of the youngsters nowadays seem to have a positive attitude towards life, and hence we see them reaching success much faster than the older generation could do. But maintaining a positive attitude in all situations is not an easy thing to do. It needs a lot of self-control, patience, and perseverance. There will be situations and circumstances that act against your will. It will cause you to lose your self-control, and you may break down. The best way to deal with it is to have a positive attitude where you deal with a bad situation by not running away from it, rather facing it with conviction and working towards changing its course by seeking an advantage from it, by taking crisis as an opportunity to prove yourself.

Let us take an example. The best example that we could take is your day-to-day work. I am sure you would have faced a situation in your workplace when you have to do the work that you don't like to do. The first reaction, or rather the natural reaction, towards it is that you will feel frustrated and you leave the frustration to build. You will get disillusioned, and you start feeling that you are not doing the right kind of job. To counter this, you should always have a positive attitude that transforms something that is not very suitable for you into something that makes you an expert in it. For instance, if your boss tells you do an administrative job while you revere to do something creative all the time, if you start hating the job given to you from the word go, you will never be able to transform it into something interesting. So the key aspect of positive attitude here would be to love the job you are doing and not find excuses for not doing it. If you go ahead and take up the administrative job and find a way to do it in a unique and better way which will actually benefit not just you but the others in the future, you have actually succeeded in applying your creative mind in doing a very ordinary job that was given to you. While it is not easy to do it all the time, it gets easier if you start seeking some kind of uniqueness in the job that you are doing, finding a better way of doing it rather than doing what you were told to do.

It is very important that you maintain it in all the situations in your life and not just your workplace. Life presents itself a more challenging situation than your job. In life you have to also deal with deep-rooted emotions. For example, let us take up a discussion between husband and wife. It is usually said that the woman is more emotional than man, but that need not be necessarily true. Both are equally emotional; however, they have different ways of showing it. Men get angry when emotions are overbearing and women cry. But the anger that men show is a more destructive force or form of energy than the crying of the women; hence, we always see that in domestic violence, men is the oppressor more often than not. So the best way to deal with life's emotions especially between husband and wife is to show a positive attitude by arguing about the reason for a difference of opinion than the difference of opinion itself. Whenever there is a situation that arises where men and women do not agree upon each other, the best way to deal with it is by trying to solve the cause than the effect. More often than not, when you show a positive attitude in looking it that way, it kind of naturally starts pointing at each other's contribution towards the difference of opinion, you start seeing your own influence in causing the difference of opinion which will be quite a revelation in itself due to which your mind calms down and you agree to solve it mutually rather than fight over it.

Therefore having a positive attitude will go a long way in making your life peaceful both at home and your office, and it works magic towards making your life more peaceful and easy to deal with rather than making it more complex and frustrating. I am sure each one of you would have faced such situation in your life. If you look back at it and see if you could have been more positive about it, you will actually see yourself in a better position than you are now.

To conclude, if you are able to maintain a balance between various critical attributes like patience, perseverance, humility, simplicity, sincerity, honesty, having a sense of achievement, being able to do the right thing all the time, living your dreams, being self-confident, empathetic, and last but not the least, having a positive attitude despite any situations and circumstances in your life, success will follow you and you will live a life of peace and prosperity. You will definitely continue to face difficulties; however, if you keep the above mentioned attributes in balance to the best possible extent, you will convincingly overcome all the tough situations in your life and come back to track, making things easier for yourself.

CPSIA information can be obtained
at www.ICGtesting.com
Printed in the USA
BVHW071730050821
613732BV00003B/428